happiness
is overrated

OTHER BOOKS BY CUONG LU

The Buddha in Jail: Restoring Lives, Finding Hope and Freedom
Wait: A Love Letter to Those in Despair

happiness
is overrated

SIMPLE LESSONS ON FINDING
MEANING IN EACH MOMENT

Cuong Lu

SHAMBHALA

Shambhala Publications, Inc.
2129 13th Street
Boulder, Colorado 80302
www.shambhala.com

© 2023 by Cuong Lu

Cover art and design: Katrina Noble
Interior design: Katrina Noble

9 8 7 6 5 4 3 2

Printed in Canada

Shambhala Publications makes every effort to print on acid-free, recycled paper.
Shambhala Publications is distributed worldwide by Penguin Random House, Inc., and its subsidiaries.

LIBRARY OF CONGRESS CATALOGING-IN-PUBLICATION DATA
Names: Lu, Cuong, 1968– author.
Title: Happiness is overrated: simple lessons on finding meaning in each moment / Cuong Lu.
Description: Boulder: Shambhala, 2023.
Identifiers: LCCN 2022025978 | ISBN 9781645471677 (trade paperback)
Subjects: LCSH: Truth—Religious aspects—Buddhism. | Four Noble Truths. | Buddhism and psychoanalysis.
Classification: LCC BQ4255 .L83 2023 | DDC 294.3/42—DC23/eng/20220622
LC record available at https://lccn.loc.gov/2022025978

Is there a difference between happiness and inner peace? Yes. Happiness depends on conditions being perceived as positive; inner peace does not.

—ECKHART TOLLE

All that is necessary to awaken to yourself . . .
[is] to turn your attention inward
to the awake silence that you are.

—ADYASHANTI

DEDICATION

I met Thich Nhat Hanh at a retreat in the Netherlands when I was eighteen. I was born during the Vietnam War, and when I came to him, I brought deep-seated fear, anger, and war. He saw that right away and taught me how to breathe consciously and walk mindfully to end the war within and touch the wonders of life. Seven years later I became a monk at Plum Village, and I stayed for sixteen years. Studying with Thich Nhat Hanh gave me new life.

Thich Nhat Hanh worked his whole life bringing mindfulness to the world. He had a special gift for explaining the deepest elements of Buddhist teachings in everyday language, which made it easy to integrate into daily life. For him, mindfulness itself was the living Dharma. He explained how to practice with a peaceful and gentle smile.

Now he is no longer with us. He passed away in January 2022, a painful loss for me. I practiced under his guidance for thirty-five years, and he helped transform a lost and fearful child into a peaceful adult and teacher. During his funeral ceremony, I made a silent promise: *You can rest now, my teacher. I promise to continue your work.*

Mindfulness helps us to be awake and to celebrate life, but it is through the wisdom of *interbeing,* a term he introduced, that we can see that happiness and suffering are one. Both are rooted in raw mind, the mind that knows no discrimination. Once you touch raw mind, you can see your connection with the whole of life. I offer the teachings in this book to my teacher Thich Nhat Hanh and express my gratitude and respect to him.

CONTENTS

A NOTE TO THE READER

At the end of each chapter, I will offer a simple practice to help you *apply* that teaching. I call these "apps." Each is only fifteen minutes long, although of course you can practice for longer or shorter, as you wish. Most of them are simple, but please take the time to practice them. Simple exercises can be transformative. They may break the spell of your usual perspective, guide you back to body and mind, and little by little, help you find yourself.

happiness
is overrated

1

Finding Myself

In 1997, I was a young monk visiting the United States for the first time, one of fifty Plum Village monastics accompanying Thich Nhat Hanh to support the practice of mindfulness with our American friends. At a daylong retreat at Spirit Rock Meditation Center in Northern California, it was my responsibility to lead the "apple meditation," to sit in front of two thousand Americans in an open field and describe how to take each bite of an apple slowly and mindfully, to really taste it and *be one* with the apple's flavor and nutrients. A local organic farmer had donated two thousand apples, and when it was time for the meditation to begin, the program coordinator, my elder sister in the Dharma, couldn't find me.

She looked and looked, and when she saw me at last, she said, "I've been trying to find you." And I spontaneously replied, "I've been trying to find myself."

I spent sixteen years as a monk at Plum Village in France trying to find myself, and I couldn't. I suffered a lot during those years, and when I left the monastery, I felt as if I'd accomplished nothing. Then one night, a year after leaving Plum Village, I awoke from a deep sleep and suddenly I understood: *I am not my emotions. I am not my concepts.* I felt completely empty, and a profound peace came over me. I was no one, not even a person.

I wanted to cry, but I stayed in deep silence enjoying the profound spaciousness inside me. After half an hour, the phone rang. It was my girlfriend, now my wife, and she said, "I feel something important is going on with you. Can you tell me what it is?" And I told her about my discovery of emptiness.

APP 1

Mindful Breathing

When I entered Plum Village, the senior monks taught me this practice: "Breathing in, I know I am breathing in.

Breathing out, I know I am breathing out." You can practice this basic mindfulness meditation while sitting on a chair and or on a cushion on the floor (or really, anyplace at any time). Follow your in-breath and your out-breath, being aware of each breath. Don't force yourself. Experience it as a game—a game of breathing and discovering life.

Find a quiet place and sit reasonably upright. Pay attention to your breathing and your whole body for ten minutes. Then pay attention to what is going on in your mind for five more minutes, just observing. Don't worry if your body fidgets. Just allow it to be itself while you are focusing on your breathing. When your mind wanders, just come back to your breathing and continue the practice. If you are overwhelmed by feelings, pause and look at your feelings with the eyes of love and compassion. This is the best practice you can do for yourself. After these fifteen minutes, see if you feel more solid. You might have a deeper sense of what is going on within and around you.

2

The Snake in the Classroom

The day I entered kindergarten, my sister and her friend walked me to school. The idea of sitting in a room full of strangers far away from home frightened me. Although the school was only five hundred yards from our house, as a five-year-old, going anywhere for a whole day without my parents was terrifying. We walked along the beach highway in our city of Nha Trang, Vietnam, and when we arrived at the schoolhouse, I began to cry. My big sister tried to reassure me: "Don't worry, Cuong. I'll go in first and kill the snake that's loose in your classroom. I'll make sure he won't bite you." I was deathly afraid of snakes, so I waited outside while she went in to slay the monster, saving my young life.

We all know my sister was lying. But at that age, I didn't know. I believed there was a big snake in the classroom. I imagined exactly where it was and what it looked like, and when I think about it now, I can still see it. It was huge and very mean. This story is stored in a place we call "mind." Every time I remember it, I feel the same fear I felt as a child. My sister is still alive, but she cannot do anything about it. She can't say, "I didn't tell you the truth. I was trying to help you be less anxious. There was no snake in your classroom." She can't help because I also know she made up that story, but *in my mind* it's a truth.

APP 2

Am I My Mind?

Stop and notice if there is some suffering in you now. Every time you suffer, you are revisiting something from the past that is coming to your mind from your mind/body/nervous system. The cause of this suffering is not just another person or whatever other external object you project your suffering onto. It comes from within.

Practice mindful breathing for five minutes: *Breathing in, I know I am breathing in. Breathing out, I know I am breathing out.* Then for ten minutes say silently, *I am here. I am in my body. I am aware of my mind.* What do you feel? Are the battles within you still raging, or are they subsiding? Do you feel better, more yourself, more the way you like to feel?

3

Connecting the Dots

My first lesson at school was to connect two points to make a line. Drawing a straight line was difficult for me; I had to repeat it hundreds of times. Finally, grasping the concept, I was proud to show the fruits of my labor to my father.

The mind *connects*. It connects us with a flower. It connects us with a loaf of bread. It connects us with feelings and ideas. We can call these connections "consciousness." We are conscious of a flower; we are conscious of a feeling; we are conscious of ideas.

In the West, we say there are five senses. According to Buddhist psychology, there are six sense consciousnesses. The first five, which we know so well, allow us to connect with the outside world of forms, sounds, smells, tastes, and tactile objects. The sixth, mind consciousness (*manovijnana*), connects us with the world inside, a world filled with ideas and feelings. The mind is the base, and these six consciousnesses are expressions of mind:

1. Our eyes see forms, and our eye consciousness identifies them, using memories and ideas that are stored in the mind as concepts.

2. Our ears hear sounds, and our ear consciousness identifies them, using memories and ideas that are stored in the mind as concepts.

3. Our nose smells odors, and our nose consciousness identifies them, using memories and ideas that are stored in the mind as concepts.

4. Our tongue tastes flavors, and our tongue consciousness identifies them, using memories and ideas that are stored in the mind as concepts.

5. Our body (body organ) touches tactile objects, and our body consciousness identifies them, using memories and ideas that are stored in the mind as concepts.

6. Our mind consciousness experiences thoughts and other ideational objects and responds to

them, using the memories and ideas that are stored in the mind as concepts. Mind consciousness can function *with* the other five consciousnesses, or it can work by itself.

We cannot draw a single straight line between the mind and any of the consciousnesses, because they're interconnected. The mind is like the ocean, and the six consciousnesses are the waves. Our minds receive data through our six sense doors and process it. When I refer to this aspect of consciousness, I use the word *mind*. It can also be called "ordinary mind." There's another part of the mind that is wild and irrational, has no beginning or end, is always present, and embraces everything. I call this "raw mind." Others have called it Buddha-nature, the womb of the Buddha, or enlightenment. From time to time, I'll use the word *mind* to refer to ordinary mind *plus* raw mind. It should be clear from the context which aspect of mind is being discussed.

Before I left Plum Village, Thich Nhat Hanh said to me, "If you find it, make it solid." He was offering a resource, but I didn't understand. Now I see that the path of practice is to move from ordinary mind to raw mind. It's a change in perspective. Now my deepest wish is to share what I've found with others. This book is my effort to do so, offering my understanding along with concrete practices. When you find raw mind, *you find yourself*.

APP 3

Am I My Six Sense Consciousnesses?

Once Thich Nhat Hanh told me, "I have arrived, I am home. That is the heart of our practice." I didn't understand what he meant. Now I do. Home is raw mind. We all need a home to come back to, a place of nondiscrimination where we are fully accepted. In raw mind, we are all equal.

Practice mindful breathing for five minutes. Then say silently, *I am aware of my five sense consciousnesses and my mind consciousness,* for ten minutes. Do you feel the connection between the "outer world" and your inner world? Do you feel as though you are arriving home, to your true home?

4

The Meaning
of an Apple

When we call something by its name, we acknowledge its *meaning*. The meaning of an apple could be to relieve hunger, produce the next generation of apples, teach us mindfulness as we savor each taste, or bring beauty into the world. Whatever it is—and it could be more than one thing—the existence of the apple is meaningful.

If you say, "Hello, Apple, you are beautiful and fragrant," that affirms its value. The same is true of you. Your name is important, and acknowledging your inherent beauty is important. When you introduce yourself, you're asserting that your life has meaning. "I am John." "I am Mary." When you say your name with confidence, others will feel your presence. And so will you.

If you think you're nobody, you won't feel respected, and you won't be able to respect others. Please respect yourself; your life is meaningful. Every morning when you wake up, call yourself by name. "Good morning, Cuong," or "Good morning, Jane." Doing this will remind you that you're important. Your very existence has meaning.

If you wake up feeling unwell, if you are truly present, your illness will have meaning. Our bodies need our care. Perhaps we need to eat healthier or do the things we enjoy or live with less stress. Illness helps us understand ourselves better, and in the process we'll understand others too. Illness has meaning.

Meaning is available in each moment of life. We can't be happy and healthy all the time. We can't be successful in every moment. Instead of focusing on success or happiness, look for meaning. When you do, you'll *find yourself*. Life is waiting to be discovered. Don't let anyone say your life is meaningless. Your life has meaning. You are important.

APP 4

Am I My Name?

Practice mindful breathing for five minutes. Then say your own name slowly, silently, over and over for ten minutes. How do you feel? More whole? More yourself?

5

True Wealth

We all want to be happy. We think happiness is the answer to every kind of suffering. Just be happy in the here and now, and everything will be fine. I wish life were that simple. But it isn't. Your happiness, for example, can be the suffering of someone else. We need to see ourselves in others, too. If we don't care about the suffering of others, that is not true happiness.

When we only think about ourselves, there are many things we can do to make ourselves happy. When we think about others, there are many things we can do to help them be happy. Sometimes, though, we need to choose. We only have one treat, and we have to choose. We can choose to eat it, or we can choose to give it to someone else. Sometimes we want to have it for ourselves, and yet we give. We're not 100 percent happy, but at a deeper level you can't overestimate the joy of giving and helping. Facing these choices is part of the journey to discovering the meaning of your life.

You are more than you think. Others are also you. When you respect others, you're respecting yourself. When you love others, you are loving yourself. When you help others, you are helping yourself. But when you're happy and others are suffering, your happiness is incomplete. When you're rich and others are poor, something is wrong. We need to share. And we need to share our happiness with those who are suffering. Only by sharing can we be truly happy. Only by sharing can we be truly wealthy. There's no way to be rich in spirit without giving and sharing.

The more you give, the richer you become. Sharing is an art. If you're rich and don't know how to share, you are still a poor person. If you are happy and don't know how to make others happy, you are suffering. Taking care of yourself is not enough. You need to learn to take care of others. Happiness is not only in the here and now. Future generations are in us. We need to work for the happiness of future generations; then we'll be happy.

In the *Lotus Sutra*, there is a story of two friends who met each other after many years apart. One had become rich, the other poor. After a dinner with a lot of alcohol, the poor friend fell soundly asleep, and the wealthy friend, before leaving, sewed a diamond inside the lining of his friend's jacket. Many years later when they met again, the poor friend was still poor. He never realized that he had a gem inside his jacket.

This is not a story about wealth. The gem is a metaphor for your true self. You have a diamond in you. You don't have to search for it; it's already yours. Happiness and suffering are both yours, as is the wisdom of knowing how precious life is. With this wisdom, we know how to love one another and protect life.

APP 5
Am I a Shade Tree, Receiving Support and Supporting Others?

Practice mindful breathing for five minutes. Then say silently, *I want to live peacefully with all beings*. Do this for ten minutes. Do you feel solid and more connected with life?

6

Knowing Your Mind

Ever since I was a little boy, I've been interested in knowing my mind. During my sixteen years as a monk, I spent most of the time observing my mind with my mind. When my mind was filled with suffering, the work was to investigate suffering. When an emotion like anger arose, I observed it.

I learned that the mind is divided into two parts: ordinary and raw. This discovery is in alignment with Abhidharma, Buddhist psychology. Ordinary mind receives information through our six sense doors and analyzes it. We store simple truths in mind like, "This is an apple," and complex truths like, "This is happiness." Some truths are transmitted by our families, culture, and education, while others we discover from our own observations and deductions. Both kinds of truth are stored in the mind as *concepts*. We have concepts about apples, happiness, hatred, and love. *Comparing* is the work of the mind. Comparing our perceptions to our concepts helps us determine if something is familiar and safe or unknown and possibly dangerous. We recognize a flower, for example, by comparing what we see or smell with the concept "flower" that is in our mind, based on education and experience. Without concepts, it would be difficult to navigate a world filled with so much information. *Recognizing* helps us feel stable.

Raw mind, on the other hand, is wild and irrational. It has no beginning, end, or continuity. It is *always* present and embraces everything. It is the source of all life. In raw mind, there's no good or bad, right or wrong. Everything simply *is*. Raw mind is a sanctuary deep within, an oasis of peace. In raw mind, there's no separation between you and me, only the seamless continuity of interbeing.

In mind, there are wars—right versus wrong, good fighting bad. The moment we discover raw mind, the wars end. This peace is not the *opposite* of war, just as right isn't the opposite of wrong or good the opposite of bad. In raw mind, we know we're all children of Mother Earth and recognize *all* beings as our brothers and sisters. To create a world where everyone lives in peace, we have to experience the depths of raw mind. We humans know how to walk on the moon, but we don't yet know how to touch our own raw minds. I hope in reading these pages and coming back to your breathing, your body, and your mind, you will feel the presence of raw mind within.

Please remember that this is not a theoretical presentation, although at times it may seem so. It's a call for peace. Understanding the mind can help us overcome suffering, ignorance, and violence. With a direct experience of raw mind, peace is possible. Raw mind is our true home, an oasis of loving-kindness beneath ordinary mind and beneath all concepts and dualities. When you touch raw mind, you find yourself.

Every step Thich Nhat Hanh took was in mindfulness, and I tried to follow his example. During another teaching tour in the United States, he said to me, "I see your steps. I know you are making every step mindfully." That made me happy and unhappy at the same time. Thich Nhat Hanh had more than mindfulness. In him, there was a profound wisdom. I knew that in my mindfulness, there was no wisdom. It looked as though we were doing the same practice, but we weren't. I was searching for something he had found.

APP 6
Am I My Views?

Practice mindful breathing for five minutes. Then say silently, *I am not my views*, for ten minutes. Is it true? If not, what is true?

7

Life's Wonders

Every object we can identify goes hand in hand with a concept, which helps us organize our experience. The concept includes the *meaning* we assign to the object. Calling an object by its name, we already have a concept of it, and that concept has meaning. Meaning is thus mind-made, and in fact, the object is mind-made, too. Many philosophers say the world is an illusion (*maya*), or mind only (*citta-matra*). They don't mean that there's no world "out there" or "in here." They mean that what we perceive and experience is as much a function of mind as it is of an empirical object, whether outer or inner. When Thich Nhat Hanh asked, "Are you sure?" he was reminding us that our perceptions have both these variables, what's "out there" and what's inside us. We always need to look again. We see what we want to see, so we often see the concepts in our mind and not the actual object. To see things as they are, we must include the perceiver, the perceived, and the perceiving.

When we slow down and look deeply, we aren't limited by dated meanings and tired concepts. If we pause, we may be able to see what is true within *and* without. Perceiving with presence is called "mindfulness." With mindfulness, we have a chance to see each object anew. Life is never fixed; only concepts are fixed. If we want change, we need to be aware of the role that concepts and meaning play in perception and then look again.

Gaze up at the sky and *feel* whether it has meaning. Look again and again until you are encountering it for the first time. Then give it a name. You might call it "blue sky." The name doesn't have to be original, but the *seeing* does. When you see and name not out of habit but out of interest, the sky will never be the same again. It will have new meaning, and you gave birth to it. When you look at everything as though for the first time, you'll never be bored. And if you do feel bored, that's okay. Sometimes we feel bored.

We can practice with the world within, too; the world under our skin that includes sensations, emotions, ideas, and wounds. The world inside is also waiting to be discovered. When you see as though for the first time, you *may* find that an unpleasant feeling isn't unpleasant at all. Just feeling things as they are can in itself be satisfying, even if difficult. Look through the eyes of an artist and see if you can discover new meaning in it. Making meaning is a way to connect the dots.

APP 7
Am I New in Each Moment?

Practice mindful breathing for five minutes. Then come back to your body and feelings, and say, silently, *I am new in each moment,* for ten minutes. Or if you'd prefer, use your own words. After these fifteen minutes, what do you feel? Do you feel refreshed? Do habits seem to have less of a hold on you? Do you feel that your life has meaning?

8

Education

Most schools teach children to build a scaffolding with words and ideas to support ordinary mind. It's important to teach our children to recognize objects and learn the names of feelings and material things. Naming and recognizing are civilizing. The more children practice this, the more they learn to function in the world.

At the same time, we must not underestimate the fluidity of a young, raw mind. A child's mind is far less closed than that of most adults, and as we teach children to name and recognize things, sadly they become less creative. Eventually they learn only to repeat what they already "know." The painter Claude Monet said, "To see, we must forget the name of the thing we are looking at," and there are spiritual practices that discourage naming in order to open new channels of insight.

Knowledge can be an obstacle. You believe you know something and cannot let go of it. Thich Nhat Hanh said that in situations like that, even if the truth comes knocking on your door, you won't let it in. We need to let go of what we already know if we want to find wisdom. "Not-knowing" can open your mind and your heart. Schools are not just places for accumulating knowledge. Schools can be places for discovering how much we don't know. A good teacher inspires us to look again.

Knowing is nice, but letting go of knowing is a true gift. There are no repeats in life; every moment is new. When we are free of preconceptions, we are able to see every person as a buddha. When I practiced this with people in prisons, they were able to feel that they were indeed buddhas. Until then, they'd looked at themselves through the lens of other people's judgments. You can't describe anything as either/or. It's never that simple. No one is good; no one is bad. We are all works in progress. We are all equal.

In spiritual education, we ask ourselves, "Who am I?" "What is love?" or "What is anger?" When love is in our heart, we can feel it. A feeling is not a concept. What does love (or anger) feel like? Write down what you discover, and later when you read your words, you will discover something new about yourself. When we're humble, we can learn something new about ourselves every day.

Raw mind is free of concepts, and its capacity for creativity is unlimited. Our educational systems need to find a balance between knowledge and discovery—opening to what *is*, encouraging surprise, and not just putting things in boxes. In raw mind, there are no judgments. We're open to the world; everything is new. When we adults look into the eyes of a child, we see innocence. Prejudice has to be learned. As soon as a child (or an adult) "knows" something, they begin to pay attention only to the boxes of their mind, disconnecting from raw mind's native wisdom. To unburden children and adults from their suffering, we need to show them how to return to raw, creative mind. In my mind, this is the most important education.

APP 8
Am I My Judgments?

Practice mindful breathing for five minutes. After that, say, silently, *I am not my judgments*, for ten minutes. Is it true?

9

Studying with a Teacher

had been a novice monk for three years when Thich Nhat Hanh asked me to write a letter of aspiration, the first step toward full ordination. In the letter, I wrote, "I will help people find their roots," although I hadn't found my own roots yet, so I didn't exactly understand what those words meant.

Not long after that, I was ordained a *bhikshu,* a fully ordained monk. As a bhikshu, my only aspiration was to realize freedom, to find my true self and to discover my roots and my true mind. With true mind—raw mind— we overcome dualistic thinking and see the true nature of things. Mindfulness helps us find our raw mind.

The best spiritual teachers do not give their students knowledge. They take "knowing" away, freeing the student's mind to perceive and experience things as they are. When we don't "know" what something is, we can *experience* it instead of suppressing or compartmentalizing it. Doing this, we discover the world and ourselves. In raw mind, we encounter everything as if for the first time, new and uncontaminated.

If we believe there is a Truth (with a capital *T*) that's absolute, it's a fallacy. There's always something we don't know, and there are things no one knows. When I began work as a chaplain, prisoners of many different faiths came to me. If they had a Truth inside them, I did not disturb it. But if I had had a Truth, it would have made it impossible for me to help. To help someone, you must be free of your Truth. Then you can share *true space*. When appropriate, I used the word *God* or *Allah* to communicate with prisoners. We connect with people where they are.

To enter the path of wisdom, the first question is, "Of what am I ignorant?" Don't be afraid of not knowing or making mistakes. We can learn from mistakes, and when we do, wisdom is there. A wise person knows their ignorance. We can even say, "Ignorance is wisdom."

Every time you make a mistake, try saying to yourself, *I've made a mistake, and I'm learning from it*. Practicing this, you return to your original wisdom.

We live with greed, anger, and ignorance. Greed makes us overconsume—food and so many other things. Anger creates wars. And ignorance drives us in the direction of racial hatred and climate change. With the change in the world's atmosphere and the extinction of so many species, our planet is out of balance. Only wisdom can stop our overconsuming and discriminating.

Wisdom begins with conscious breathing. If you practice conscious breathing every morning before you go to work or school and before going to bed at night, your life will change, and life on earth will change. Mindfulness practice helps bring us in the direction of raw mind, where we can live together in love and respect.

In 2000, I received the lamp transmission from Thich Nhat Hanh and was recognized by him as a teacher. After the ceremony, Thich Nhat Hanh said to me, "This is only the beginning. You need another ten years to reach the goal, to be a real Zen teacher." His estimate turned out to be correct. I found raw mind ten years later. The moment I found myself, I found my teacher. I realized that I *am* my teacher, there is no distance between us.

The Dharma I received from my teacher was not his invention. It was transmitted from the Buddha to Zen master Nhat Dinh (1784–1847), the first abbot of Tu Hieu Pagoda, Thich Nhat Hanh's home temple in central Vietnam, and he transmitted it to me. Now I want to share it with you, with love, respect, and trust.

APP 9

Am I Free?

Practice mindful breathing for five minutes. Then say silently, *I am free*. Do this for ten minutes. Do you feel inspired to look again for what keeps you imprisoned and how you can go deeper and find the real peace and true goodness that exclude nothing?

10

Four Noble Truths

In the first sermon he gave after his enlightenment the Buddha said, "There are two kinds of wars in us: fighting suffering and seeking happiness. My teachings can free you from both wars." He also said, "It's never too late to end your greed, hate, and delusion." Then he taught the Four Noble Truths as the path from suffering to true happiness.

The first truth is *dukkha satya*. *Dukkha* means "suffering," and *satya* means "truth," so literally "the truth of suffering." He did not suggest that we deny, gloss over, or filter our suffering through a happy lens. He called suffering a "noble truth" (*arya satya*), and he encouraged us to look deeply into it to see it clearly.

The second noble truth the Buddha taught is *dukkha samudaya*, which means that suffering has a *cause*. Here he encouraged us to look for the source of our suffering. Some people suggest that craving is the cause, but the Buddha and his successors used craving as one example of possible causes, not the only cause of all suffering. Later Buddhist teachers noted that there are always multiple causes of suffering, or of anything, never just one. Knowing there are causes encourages inner exploration to find them.

Looking at the first truth (suffering), we see the second truth (cause). It's not about finding someone to blame. A primary cause of suffering is the way we look at life. It's about mind. Our way of looking is inherently incomplete and thus erroneous. All of our concepts are outdated. They may have been helpful when we discovered them, but then they become a habit. If we can see our habit of associating this with that, of putting things in a box, we begin to have the insight that can free us from our dated, counterproductive ways of looking. Even after a great discovery when we feel a burden lifted and our suffering lessened, we aren't done. When the next experience of suffering comes, we'll need to do it again.

The third noble truth is *dukkha nirodha*, which means "the cessation of suffering," referring to the cessation of the rearising of our concepts about anything. This noble truth is about freedom: with honest and clear perception, we can free ourselves from our suffering. This is the good news. There are seeds of happiness in our suffering, and seeds of suffering in our happiness. The third noble truth is about raw mind.

The fourth noble truth is *dukkha nirodha marga*, or the "path to end suffering." When the Buddha says in the first noble truth that there is suffering, he is talking about the way our minds work. In the fourth noble truth, he offers eight practices known as the Eightfold Path that can free us from the habits that keep us from touching life: right view, right thinking, right speech, right action, right livelihood, right diligence, right attention, and right concentration. Together, these eight are the practice of mindful living. In ordinary mind, suffering is the enemy of happiness. In raw mind, suffering is just suffering.

Suffering has a purpose. By understanding someone's suffering, you understand what they need in order to be happy. Peace is not made by happiness alone. It is made by nondiscrimination toward happiness and suffering. We don't practice mindfulness to have only peaceful experiences. Thich Nhat Hanh said that to touch wisdom, we need to "look deeply." Buddhist meditation has two parts: stopping and looking deeply. Mindful breathing helps us stop and see what's going on in our body and mind. That's an important point of entry.

Am I My Suffering?

Practice mindful breathing for five minutes. Then say silently, *I know suffering is present.* When you practice this, you may feel some of the ways suffering is part of your life. If you can, do it for ten minutes. If ten minutes is too long, practice for a few minutes or a few seconds. It is important that you not fight against your suffering. Your suffering needs understanding. It won't help to ignore it or fight against it. If it's too much to do this alone, when you feel ready you can explore your suffering with a therapist, a spiritual teacher, or a health-care professional.

11

Suffering Is Not Enough

In his classic book *Being Peace,* Thich Nhat Hanh writes, "Life is filled with suffering, but it is also filled with many wonders. . . . To suffer is not enough. We must also be in touch with the wonders of life." As a monk, I saw happiness as something to "get." It felt as if success in the practice was being measured by how much happiness we had. If we weren't happy, we were told that we weren't practicing correctly. So I looked for happiness under every stone and in every breath. Practices like mindful breathing and living joyfully in community were offered, but they didn't work for me. I was looking for happiness in all the wrong places—starting with "the present moment."

The present moment means wholeness, not rejecting anything. But I was looking for "the present moment" as a *concept,* as though there is really such a "time." I didn't understand *interbeing*, the web of connectivity among beings, time, and space, or that the true roots of suffering are mistaking the formations of mind for the objects they represent.

Thousands of inspirational books teach us how to overcome suffering and attain happiness. Some say, "The way out is through," encouraging us to *feel* our suffering. Others suggest transcending suffering, standing above and viewing it from an aerial perspective. Many suggest supplanting suffering with happiness. In Buddhism, this is called "replacing the peg." They're all valuable, but they did not relieve my suffering. I held on tightly to the concepts of happiness and the present moment.

Emotions are composed of feelings and concepts. To avoid being swept away by an emotion, we think we need a concept to contain it. When we feel an emotion, we compare it to an idea or some meaning we already have, afraid that otherwise things might get out of control. So we avoid feeling what is and stick to the concepts we produce in our mind. Suffering is the discrepancy between truth and ideation, between what is and what we wish or believe.

Practicing conscious breathing brought me a certain amount of peace. I transformed conceptual suffering into conceptual peace. But a concept is not the thing itself; it's just a way of compartmentalizing. Ultimately, all emotions are mind-made, and there's no difference between one and another. The way to happiness is to understand that all concepts are produced by mind and they are all equal. We can treat all our emotions with respect, whether we are experiencing joy, love, anger, or hatred. We don't discriminate. For many years I didn't know that, and I suffered.

When I discovered raw mind, I saw that we are all empty of good and bad. Generally, we think, speak, and act based on ideas of good and bad. I tried hard to be a good monk, and my practice led me to pride and ignorance. Discovering raw mind has freed me from pride, and for the first time, I can be myself.

In true wisdom, there is always humility. No one is better than anyone else. No species is better than another. I was a proud monk, and the harder I practiced, the prouder I became. My teacher tried to teach me the wisdom of nondiscrimination and the insight of inter-being, but I didn't understand. A year after I left Plum Village, I discovered that no one has a monopoly on wisdom, that true wisdom belongs to everyone. I think that's what Thich Nhat Hanh was trying to tell me.

APP 11
Am I Ever-Deepening Wisdom?

Practice mindful breathing for five minutes. Then say silently, *When I make a mistake, I can learn from it. I see the innate wisdom of each mistake*. Do this for ten minutes and see what happens.

12

Real Happiness

For sixteen years in Plum Village, I tried to find happiness, and the more I looked for it, the more I suffered. Monastic practice was difficult for me. It was only later, when I discovered that real happiness doesn't have a cause, that I understood the efforts of my elder brothers and sisters in the Dharma. Happiness cannot have a cause, because it's not a concept. True happiness can only be found when you encounter emptiness.

I wanted to be happy and respected, seen as intelligent, and I did everything I could to reach that goal. But instead I discovered that the more you cultivate your "good" traits, the stronger your "bad" traits get. They go hand in hand. That's the law of consciousness. Good and bad are two sides of the same coin. Thich Nhat Hanh did everything he could to help, and I did everything I could, but I was proud as a monk and unable to discover these simple truths in that field of pride. After sixteen years, I left the monastery. I knew it had been an ideal environment, and yet I wasn't able to find myself there. I had invested my prime years in monastic life and left feeling like a failure.

My first year outside the monastery was difficult. It took time to get used to being in society. Then I had the profound experience I described in chapter 1, and for a moment, I was free of all the ideas I had about myself. I saw that I was neither good nor bad, existent nor nonexistent, and for the first time, I felt free.

A year later, I was hired by the government of the Netherlands to be a prison chaplain. When I began, most of the prisoners were unable to sit still long enough to listen to my talks. They kept interrupting. But in a short time, they learned to sit quietly, and soon they were inviting other prisoners to join the meditations. I told them they are not separate from their ancestors and their families, and many of them were smiling and crying. They were there, I felt, looking for the happiness they'd never found, and it was deeply satisfying to watch them making such a deep and sincere effort. Oddly enough, prison offered them a chance to experience real happiness.

What surprised me most was not what I was able to offer them, but what the prisoners were able to offer me. They confirmed for me that happiness is a truth, that happiness and suffering are very close to each other, and that touching our own suffering can be a source of relief and even a prerequisite for true happiness.

It seemed miraculous that I was able to connect so quickly with men society considered to be hardened criminals. Perhaps my upbringing in a war zone prepared me for this moment, and I was able to meet them in their pain and, together, touch what is deep and true. Many of these prisoners suffered because of judgments—good and bad, right and wrong. They were lost in these judgments and couldn't see the way back to themselves. And if they were not themselves, they'd never have a chance to get in touch with their true, essential goodness—raw mind—which is present in each of us. When I sat with them, I didn't have an idea that I was a chaplain or that they were prisoners. We touched each other's hearts, free from concepts. We can't control concept generation, but we can see the process and deconstruct the notions upon which our judgments are based.

APP 12

Am I a Source of Wisdom Supporting All Beings?

Practice mindful breathing for five minutes. Then say silently, *I am a leaf of a tree, and I am the roots nourishing the leaves*. Do this for ten minutes. Do you feel solid and happy?

13

Feeling Safe

When I came to the West as an eleven-year-old, I could not connect with others—or with life. I was afraid of everyone. As a child of war, I could still feel the war in my body. I felt small in a big world. The war in Vietnam had ended, but the war inside came with me. The primary function of ordinary or conceptual mind is discrimination. Mind *distinguishes* good from bad, right from wrong, birth from death, and you from me—to help us feel safe. As a new arrival in the West, I was using this function of mind to turn against myself. I was in pain and afraid, and I isolated myself.

To overcome discrimination—against yourself or another person—begin by acknowledging that suffering is present (the first noble truth). "I see that you're suffering," or "I see that I'm suffering." When you do, connection is already there. The object of discrimination (you yourself or the other person) will experience your loving compassion. Suffering is still present, but wisdom is there too. Loving-kindness leavens the situation. When things aren't going well, you can sit quietly, without judgment, and try to understand yourself and others. In that situation, love sometimes arises naturally.

By its very nature, thinking is repetitious. There are few, if any *new* thoughts. When life is reduced to a thought or a prejudice, it's already old. Thoughts are formed from older thoughts, most of which come from other people, not from our own experience. How do we stop thinking or feeling? That's not the point. What we can do is stop discriminating between good and bad, right and wrong, inside and outside, ourselves and others. Discrimination, which is the basis of ordinary mind, prevents us from touching reality, where things *are* as they are. Try to stop thinking for ten minutes. I've done it; it's possible. If you do, you'll have a very different understanding of concepts.

Even the thought of happiness, when repeated, brings suffering. True happiness is not a thought. We can never catch reality with a concept. We believe the mind can store memories, but all memories are incomplete. We need to pay attention to actual suffering instead of clinging to memories. When we stay present with our actual suffering, we'll discover real happiness.

Trying to hold on to anything comes from fear. We want something to hold on to, so we don't have to be so afraid. I've tried this, and it doesn't work. The only way to overcome fear is to accept everyone and everything, to see each person as your sister or brother, your parent, or your child. Even before we're born, we are already "everyone." We don't then become separate. My deepest dream is for people to realize that we're all one family manifesting in many forms and colors, so we'll learn to stop discriminating and live peacefully together on the earth.

Children understand that they don't exist outside each other. We need education in nondiscrimination so we stop imagining differences where there are none, and we stop creating divisions based on concepts and then judging others based on whether they are inside or outside, good or bad. Can we create an educational system based on nondiscrimination and experiential insight? To do this, we need teachers who embody this insight. When we base our actions on nondiscrimination, we contribute to peace. When we're afraid of others, we believe the way to have peace is to separate and isolate, which includes censoring texts that aren't in alignment with our preconceptions. When we touch wisdom—fearlessly dwelling in boundless, raw mind—we don't need to censor books or transform others. The only thing we need to be afraid of is our discriminating mind. That's what gives rise to division, hatred, and violence. We need the wisdom of equality, which comes from understanding. This insight is in each of us, in our raw mind.

APP 13

Am I My Mind?

Practice mindful breathing for five minutes. Then say silently, for ten minutes, *My mind is always new and fresh.* Do you feel more at ease?

14

Equanimity

Happiness is overrated. It's not better than suffering. It's the other side of the same coin. In the Four Noble Truths, the Buddha teaches that happiness and suffering are equal. Ordinary mind differentiates between happiness and suffering and has its ups and downs. Raw mind sees happiness and suffering with equanimity and remains neutral about it all. To attain happiness is not to move from suffering to happiness. Enlightenment is not a giddy state of ebullience or a zombie-like state of flatness. It is being alive, feeling happiness when it is present and feeling suffering when that is our plight.

Most people see the Four Noble Truths as a problem-solving technique. I don't think this is correct. Suffering is not a problem to be solved. It is a truth to be recognized. Ordinary mind tries to avoid suffering, so it takes work and practice to stay present with, feel, and understand suffering. When we *recognize* suffering, we touch the first noble truth. When we stay present with suffering, feeling it and not being carried away by it, we touch the fourth noble truth. This is the practice of equanimity. It's not easy. Enter the world of equanimity slowly, or you will be unable to feel the difference between genuine equanimity and simply shutting down.

The first and fourth noble truths are the same coin—tails is recognition and heads is staying present and not running away. Suffering is not an obstacle to a meaningful life. On the contrary, suffering can help you understand the world, and attachment to happiness can be an obstacle. If we hold on tightly to what we have, our curiosity may not be ignited. Suffering shakes us up. It makes us look again and engenders reevaluation. To get through difficulties, we have to wake up, and we can learn a lot in the process. When we are forced to move beyond the confines of our circumscribed life, we touch reality more deeply and long only for meaning.

Laurens van der Post wrote, "There is ultimately only one thing that makes human beings deeply and profoundly bitter, and that is to have thrust upon them a life without meaning. . . . There is nothing wrong in searching for happiness. But of far more comfort to the soul is something greater than happiness or unhappiness, and that is meaning."

In the Buddha's mind model, he suggests practicing equanimity in the presence of both happiness and suffering, to see things as they are and not run away. Staying with our suffering to the extent that we can (take breaks when you need to) helps us grapple with life's biggest questions. When I was a prison chaplain, I saw that those who touched their own *real suffering* felt profoundly happy afterward. Touching any experience, even those that are painful, is more satisfying than suppression or avoidance.

Because suffering makes us feel fragmented and unstable, ordinary mind works 24/7 to transform it into happiness. Ordinary mind gifts us with a pair of rose-tinted glasses that color everything and help us cope with conflicts and instability. That is the purpose of this filter—to keep us from touching reality. Sometimes we need them; the reality is too destabilizing. We need to know our limits and proceed at a pace that we (and our spiritual teacher or therapist or guide) feel is right for us. Touching suffering without a filter can be intolerable at times, so titrate; do it in small doses. Eventually, touching raw suffering is a way to transform pain not by removing it as such but by seeing its true perspective, meaning, and function. We don't need to replace our suffering with happiness or any other filtered concept. We need guidance and support to stay with our unfiltered suffering.

Everybody suffers. The question is, do we suffer with or without insight? Some people eat to be happy. Some people use alcohol to avoid suffering. Some people use drugs; some play on their smartphones or watch TV in a kind of trance. We each have our own methods, which we then perfect. When we suffer without insight, the suffering can be terrible, and so of course, we try to avoid or numb it. But when we are able to stay present with our suffering, when we know what our suffering is, we aren't afraid of it. Suffering is a part of life.

APP 14
Am I Nonfear?

Practice mindful breathing for five minutes. Then say silently, *Suffering is not an obstacle*. Do this for ten minutes and see if your life feels more meaningful.

15

Being and Nonbeing

One day after studying existentialism, I went out for a walk. Along the path were rows of beautiful tulips, and I turned to one of them and asked, "Are you a flower?"

"No," she replied spontaneously. "I'm coming apart. Don't you see my petals dropping?"

"But if you're not a flower, what are you?"

"Sir, I am neither being nor nonbeing."

"Wow," I thought, "Jean-Paul Tulipe."

Mind categorizes things as "being" or "nonbeing," existent or nonexistent. The concept of nonbeing is based on the concept of being. Both are stored in mind and are inherently inaccurate. Ideas and concepts are never the things themselves; they're representations to help us *recognize* what we see, think, and feel. They're maps drawn from the past so we have something to compare our experience to. When we say, "I am" or "the flower is," we think it's true. But words are a manifestation of mind. Upon deeper reflection, I couldn't put the tulip into either of these categories: being or nonbeing. To understand a flower—or anything—we need to go deeper than mind.

We look for an "I," a "you," and a "tulip," and when we find them, we think we're separate, and we feel lonely. As scientists, we're trying to see patterns and find order in the universe, but since the Big Bang, our universe has always been chaotic.

If we see ourselves as existent, we may feel anxious that, at some point, we'll die and become nonexistent. This is a *view*—a view that something that exists now will someday cease to exist. Like all views, it's not real. We coexist with all other beings, and we will forever. We're not time bound or limited to our "selves." If you see yourself as a separate, stand-alone being, that is not correct. Your parents are in you—whether you get along with them or not. All your ancestors are in you. And society is in you, too. You can't take society out of you.

Being suggests not only permanence but also separateness, both of which are impossible. We're always changing, and we're always connected with everything. We cannot be separate, and so *being* cannot describe reality. Your nature is neither being nor nonbeing. If it were nonbeing, you wouldn't exist. That's what nonbeing means.

We are a witness to nonstop fighting among dualistic concepts, because we forget they all share the same base and therefore are all equal. The base of all concepts is emptiness. Each being and every nonbeing are based in emptiness. We think things are on their way to becoming something else, but they're really just moving. It's impossible to catch anything and label it as being or nonbeing.

Look in the mirror. You'll see *your* face. But your face is also my face. Your body is also my body. We inter-are, and this perspective frees us from the view that we are only ourselves. We are *everything*. If you love someone, you are loving yourself. And if you discriminate against someone, you are discriminating against yourself. We are all colors and all races. We are the whole cosmos— the earth, the sun, the stars, the rain, the forest, and the mountains. Sit quietly on a chair or a cushion or directly on the ground and follow each breath in and out. Imagine yourself as a mountain, solid and fluid at the same time. We are always moving; every atom and all our cells are constantly in flux. If we live in the realm of being and nonbeing, we have happiness or suffering. If we live in raw mind, there is no duality, only connection and peace.

APP 15

Am I a Flower, a Tree, or All of Nature?

Practice mindful breathing for five minutes. Then say silently, *I am grateful for the support of all beings*. Do this for ten minutes and feel the solidity and fluidity—at the same time—of your place in the cosmos.

16

Emptiness

The idea that something either exists or doesn't is overly simplistic. I spent many years looking for a point that is *between* existence and nonexistence, as though it were the Holy Grail, the key to unlock the enigma of either/or. Then, one day as I was studying the *Heart Sutra*, I realized that the key is emptiness. In the *Heart Sutra*, Avalokiteshvara, an awakened being of great compassion, teaches the Buddha's disciple Shariputra that the cause of suffering is the expectation that things will stay the same forever. Life is never static. It *flows*. Emptiness explains this.

When you look into a teacup, you see that it is empty. Even after I fill the cup with tea, it's still empty. There may be tea in the cup for a while, but the nature of the cup is emptiness. It's not just porcelain or china. There is also empty space. Without this space, I couldn't call it a cup. Thanks to emptiness, I can pour water, milk, coffee, or apple juice into the cup too, not just tea.

Emotions are also "empty," insofar that what arises is temporary. Our emotional space may be filled with an unpleasant feeling now, but we know it will only stay for a while. Eventually it will be replaced by another feeling. Emptiness means that things are fluid, not fixed. Tea quenches thirst. Anger reveals something we need to see and feel. It's usually best if we don't act it out or push it down. We don't need to think that love or another feeling would be better. Love is empty, too; all emotions are. If we don't discriminate against anger, we won't be crushed by it. When we understand that *everything* is empty, life becomes luminous and renewable.

Thich Nhat Hanh taught, "Emptiness is always empty of something" and specifically that it is "empty of a separate self." Everything in the universe is of the nature of emptiness. When certain conditions are present, we have an apple. When they aren't, the apple becomes something else. An apple won't stay crisp forever. *Interbeing* is another word for emptiness that can help free us from being and grasping. Thich Nhat Hanh explained this as follows:

> If you are a poet, you will see clearly that there is a cloud floating in this sheet of paper. Without . . . rain, the trees cannot grow, and without trees, we cannot make paper. . . . If the cloud is not here, the sheet of paper cannot be here either. So we can say the cloud and the paper *inter-are*. . . . When Avalokita says that our sheet of paper is empty, he means it is empty of a separate, independent existence. It cannot just be by itself. It has to inter-be with the sunshine, the cloud, the forest, the logger, the mind, and everything else. . . . Empty of a separate self means full of everything.*

Emptiness is not a thing. Interbeing is not a truth. They are concepts, ways of understanding. They explain something elusive and put all other teachings—self/not-self, being/nonbeing, and so on—in perspective.

* Thich Nhat Hanh, *The Heart of Understanding: Commentaries on the Prajnaparamita Heart Sutra* (Berkeley: Parallax Press, 1988), 3, 10.

Although each of us is an individual, we are also undivided. Uniqueness and interconnection arise from the same root. We are all deeply connected. One day, I was sitting in the garden with Thich Nhat Hanh, near a bed of Italian red poppies. He looked at me and said, "These flowers are impermanent. That's why they're so beautiful."

APP 16
Am I Life and Death?

Practice mindful breathing for five minutes. Then say silently, *Understanding death, I live my life with ease*. Do this for ten minutes. Do you feel more rooted in life?

17

Giving and Receiving

I met Thich Nhat Hanh when I was nineteen. As he walked into the meditation hall at a retreat center in the Netherlands, he radiated peace. He said, "I am sixty years old," and we all spontaneously applauded. He looked so young and so peaceful. Then he began to talk about conscious breathing. "Breathe and smile," he said. After the talk, he taught us walking meditation, being mindful of your steps and your breathing while walking.

I could see that Thich Nhat Hanh was *really alive*. He lived deeply in every moment, and for the first time, I felt I was in the presence of someone who understood life's meaning. When we touch the meaning of life, we want to serve others in the way a mother cares for her children. We do it out of love, and when we experience that, we have found the meaning of life. He had discovered his true self. Until you discover your real self, life lacks meaning. It begins to make sense when you can support others. We need to give and to receive. We need other people and nonpeople too. If we think only of ourselves, we won't survive.

A teacher can be a "way-shower," someone who gives guidance and support and helps us see our way. A teacher can help you open your mind. I knew immediately that he was my teacher. My father had passed away four years earlier, and I felt rudderless not having an elder to guide me. Encountering Thich Nhat Hanh was like meeting my father again. I blended my father and teacher into one person. A teacher is a root, connecting us to all the teachers who have ever walked the earth. As a teacher myself now, I try to help students connect with their roots, their own true homes.

When I became a monk, my friends thought I was crazy. I ran into one of them recently, and he reminded me how surprised he had been when he learned I was moving to Plum Village. He thought I was ending the sweet dream of my life. Coming from a poor country like Vietnam, we saw the West as a dreamland. We were able to study at the best universities and explore the newest ideas in the world. To him, I was running away from life. No one understood my decision, but I couldn't have made any other. I had found my teacher and connected with my roots.

In the summer of 2018, I traveled with a group of my students to Vietnam, and we went to Yen Tu Mountain, where Tran Nhan Tong, a great emperor who became a monk, lived and practiced seven hundred years ago. I gave a talk there, and during the talk one of my students touched her own deep roots. She saw me there, and to her I represented all the ancestors, blood and spiritual, of the past seven hundred years, and she wept. In each of us, there is a true teacher always trying to help us find ourselves.

When I was a novice monk, I naively asked Thich Nhat Hanh, "Have you done anything better than the Buddha?" And he replied confidently, "The Buddha would have done what I'm doing if he had lived in the twenty-first century. I don't see any separation between the Buddha and me." The living teachings are transmitted from generation to generation, and each generation of teachers has to express the teachings anew. That way they are not simply repeated but renewed.

Am I Future Generations?

Practice mindful breathing for five minutes. Then say silently for ten minutes, *I am the next seven generations*. Do you feel more connected to the earth and all beings?

18

Self-Consciousness

Buddhist psychology describes a function of mind it calls *manas*. Manas is self-centered, a little grabby in its efforts to create for us a world that feels safe and continuous. When we experience anything, manas reaches into the *alayavijnana* (consciousness's storehouse or seed bin), where all concepts and potentialities are "stored."

Manas then fetches concepts that can help us make sense of that particular experience. This is how we navigate the world. Each concept is discrete, and manas's job is to connect the dots—the concepts, or "seeds"—and craft an autobiography from small packets of memories. Because concepts are never the thing itself, our *interpretations* of what we experience are inherently inaccurate.

In composing these stories, manas conjures a permanent self—"I am," "I'm right," "I'm self-important." From piecing together memories, manas interprets the experience and concocts the idea of an "I," processing billions of concepts per millisecond. When I say, "I'm Cuong," that's manas connecting the dots. Manas means well. It wants us to be safe and happy. But manas and the concepts it relies on are simply not "true." They are, at best, an approximation.

When you find yourself carried away by one of manas's interpretations and thus disconnected from your true self, you can go back to your breathing and allow your in- and out-breaths and awareness of feelings and sensations to help you return "home." Staying present with *what is*, you are much more likely to feel satisfaction. Not-knowing is a good place to start. To see things as they are, we begin by letting go of views, which are manas's interpretation of our experiences.

One time when I traveled to the United States with Thich Nhat Hanh and other Plum Village monastics, we were in Los Angeles with Zen master Man Giac, and Thich Nhat Hanh asked me to tell Thich Man Giac about the lazy days at Plum Village. I explained, "Once a week at Plum Village, we have a lazy day. There's nothing scheduled for the whole day. We wake up whenever we want and do whatever we want. We just follow our noses, and thanks to lazy days, I get to see myself from a different perspective." Thich Nhat Hanh smiled.

Thich Man Giac was the Supreme Patriarch of the Vietnamese United Buddhist Churches of America and having lazy days at a monastery was simply unheard of. Surprised, he said, "The Buddha practiced diligently for six years before he was enlightened. In Japan, where I trained, we had a practice called Six-Year Asceticism, inspired by the Buddha's quest." My teacher continued to smile, and after a while, he said, "Lazy day is a practice of high quality."

APP 18

Am I a Continuation of Yesterday?

Practice mindful breathing for five minutes. Then say silently, *I know I am new and unique,* for ten minutes. Can you taste the spacious potency of freedom that is in your heart?

19

Being Nobody, Doing Nothing

When memories are painful, we are inclined to forget what happened. So we run away from suffering toward happiness. In the Four Noble Truths, the Buddha taught that suffering has value. Feeling our suffering, if we do it carefully with the proper guidance and support, can be the doorway to awakening. Suffering helps us remember the past and become present with what is in our life now.

Mindfulness helps us stay present with suffering. We can use mindfulness to stand in the presence of suffering and see that under the light of awareness, suffering is just suffering. It has its own past, and when we feel it, we may be able to understand its source. If we honor it, it won't control us. Sometimes we need to run away. But sometimes we can stay present with it. Somatic memories have their own truths to set us free, when we are ready.

Doing nothing, simply staying present, is one way to deal with emotional challenges. Conscious breathing is an effective way of "doing nothing." Society tells us, "Don't just sit there, do something," and wisdom tells us the opposite. Without wisdom, we'd run through life like a chicken without a head, pursuing every impulse. Staying deeply present with suffering is its own form of happiness. Holding on to superficial happiness is suffering.

The prisoners I worked with were moved when they discovered that their suffering could be a source of happiness, a gateway to freedom. Staying present with what is can be cleansing. Most prisoners have challenging pasts, and they don't have much of a present either. They only have suffering. If you want to help someone who is suffering, never tell them to look for happiness. Happiness is illusory; for them, suffering is what's real.

Sometime a situation is so dark that a person doesn't want to live anymore. I understand the feeling. When all you have is suffering, it can be impossible to want to go on living. What can we do when someone who is suffering that much comes to us for help? The answer is "nothing." If you think you can do something, you're deceiving yourself and misleading the other person. The way to help is by doing nothing. All spiritual and self-help techniques encourage you, ultimately, to do nothing. The most powerful practice is simply to be present, to hold space, and in doing so, encourage others (and ourselves) to touch life again. Prisoners have come up empty-handed so many times while trying to find happiness, they understand this intuitively.

When you can stay present in the midst of your own suffering, you offer others a living teaching and a path. People who are lost need way-showers who can encourage them to stay present with themselves. Sometimes it's too much, though, and you need to take a break. Do a little—tiny steps are important—and take another break. Take a warm bath and come back later. Treat your wounds with care.

Am I My Presence?

Practice mindful breathing for five minutes. Then say silently, *I am alive. I am truly present*. Do this for ten minutes. Do you feel more awake and alive?

20

The Raft Is Not the Shore

Thich Nhat Hanh was always a playful, inventive person, seeking new ways to remind us to practice. One time at Plum Village he used a toy someone had given him—a wooden bird with a button that made a chirping sound. He put the toy in his pocket, and when we were gathered around him, he would suddenly push the button. The bird's song reminded us that we were living in forgetfulness. We all came back to our conscious breathing, and Thich Nhat Hanh smiled. His wooden bird had become our bell of mindfulness.

In the kitchen at Plum Village, we had a clock that had a quarter-hour chime. Each time it began to chime, we stopped whatever we were doing and focused on our breathing. After three mindful breaths, we continued our kitchen work. We chopped vegetables as part of our meditation practice. One time while I was dicing vegetables, Thich Nhat Hanh came into the kitchen and asked, "What are you doing, my son?" I thought, *I'm dicing vegetables*, but that couldn't be what he was asking. He could see what I was doing. So I figured the real question was, "Are you practicing presence—mindful awareness—while you are slicing?" And the honest answer was no. So I looked up and smiled. He smiled back and left the kitchen. I continued dicing, this time following my breathing at the same time.

Thich Nhat Hanh practiced wherever he was. He told me, "Even in the bathroom, practice exactly as you do in the meditation hall. Practice in a way that there's no difference between inside and outside."

One time, I entered the meditation hall behind him, and he suddenly turned and asked, "Are we inside or outside?" He didn't wait for me to answer; he had already entered the hall. I followed, but I knew I was still outside.

I had not yet entered the heart of Buddhist wisdom. My mind still divided the world into good and bad, right and wrong, inside and outside. I had a long road ahead, from my ordinary mind to raw mind.

According to the Yogachara tradition of Buddhism,* mind has three functions: remembering, thinking, and discerning. To remember is to store experiences in mind as concepts. Then, when we see, hear, smell, taste, or feel something, we compare it with the stored concept closest to that experience and feel as though we recognize it. As we now know, concepts are not the reality. Cognition is therefore always a best guess. Identifying and naming are inherently imperfect.

Even mindfulness can be a product of mind. The ideal of mindfulness practice—recognizing without judging—is next to impossible. In recognizing, there is already discerning. We're wired to discriminate for safe-

* Yogachara, literally "yoga practice," is an influential tradition of Buddhist philosophy and psychology emphasizing the study of cognition, perception, and consciousness through the interior lens of meditative and yogic practices. Yogachara doctrine is summarized in the term *vijnapti-matra*, meaning "nothing but cognition" (often rendered "consciousness only" or "mind only").

ty's sake. Understanding mind means knowing that concepts are at best reflections of truth. Literally, *smriti* (*sati* in Pali), the term translated from early Buddhist texts as *mindfulness*, means "to remember," and memory is inherently flawed.

The Buddha compared his teaching to a raft that brings travelers to the shore of awakening. I call awakening "raw mind," when our experience is unmitigated by interpretation or judgment. Raw mind is just being. The Buddha said it's important to distinguish between the raft and the shore. The raft is useful for crossing over, but we don't want to hold on to it once we've reached the shore of liberation. Letting go of the raft, letting go of concepts, being with what *is* in our body and in the world, that is *real* happiness.

APP 20

Am I at the Shore of Peace?

Practice mindful breathing for five minutes. Then say silently, *I have arrived at the shore of peace*. Do this for ten minutes. Do you feel more energy in yourself? Do you feel alive?

21

Stillness

Stillness is not the absence of noise or even the absence of suffering. In stillness, everything is present. Everything has its place. We feel suffering, but we don't experience it as "mine" or even as "suffering." Real happiness cannot be possessed. It is *inter-happiness*. The more we share it, the stronger it becomes. It is peace without borders, embracing everything. Inter-happiness doesn't belong to anyone; we all benefit from it. When we believe happiness has limits, when we see life from the perspective of a self, we miss the chance to enjoy life's wonders. Stillness—the absence of a separate self—is filled with wonder.

Stillness helps us see how strong we are. In raw mind, which could be called "one mind" or "no mind," there is no separation. Nor is there birth or death. Dwelling in raw mind, we live more deeply, completely in balance. We do not deny our existence. We do not reject our uniqueness. In this stillness, we exist and we're unique. We're ourselves, and we are happy.

In stillness, the balance between happiness and suffering, life and death, you and others is restored. Trying to avoid suffering doesn't make life easier. It tilts us out of balance. Being in balance is more satisfying than being happy. True happiness is always balanced with suffering.

Mindfulness can help us be peaceful and happy. Our ordinary mind can be noisy and restless, and we want the noise to go away. We want everything in life to be comfortable and well-organized. We see stress as the enemy and want calmness all the time. But the Buddha said that suffering is a truth. He did not say that it's the enemy. Suffering needs to be respected. Avoiding stress can be a missed opportunity for change.

The Vietnamese emperor-monk Tran Nhan Tong wrote, "Although my body is in the city, my mind is dwelling in the forest." Connecting with nature is one way we can find real happiness. Take a walk in the woods or swim in a lake. Do you feel a peace beyond words? Sometimes it's so quiet that our mental activities seem to stop. If we felt separate from the environment before, we don't anymore. In stillness, there is no separation between us and raw mind, or between you and me. Everything becomes clear. Past, present, and future dissolve into timelessness.

Am I Peace?

Practice mindful breathing for five minutes. Then say silently, *Beneath the fray, I am peaceful and happy*. Do this for ten minutes. Do your heart and mind feel in balance? Are you able to touch the stillness beneath the fray?

22

Freedom

Ordinary mind is, by nature, dualistic. Everything conditioned is born, and it dies. It becomes more and then it becomes less. When "goodness" comes to mind, we may become attached to it and want it to stay forever, but it's neither stable nor permanent. One day it's goodness, the next day it's badness, or even evil. All are concepts that share the same base, which is dualistic mind. They are always paired with an "I" concept. We may believe "I am good" or "I'm right," but rightness can never be possessed. When we think we're good and others are bad, we hurt everyone. When we're attached to "one truth," we suffer. Raw mind is *free* of truth. In a united, peaceful world, there's no inside or outside, no separation at all.

When you hurt someone, you want to repair the damage. Restoration is a wholesome act. At the same time, we know that in raw mind, even ignorance is not less than wisdom. Good and evil have the same value. Right and wrong have the same value. In mind they are enemies, but in raw mind they are sibs.

When we've been hurt, we build up hatred. Hatred isn't wrong or evil. In some religions, we're taught to show only love and compassion. But anger and hatred have their place. We can strive for goodness and happiness, but we also need space for evil and ignorance. Being honest is what's important. That is the key to peace. In hatred, there is also love. In raw mind, love and hatred are not enemies. We have to look at our wounds and not pretend everything is okay. We are all wounded. We've all hurt others, and we are not 100 percent good. We need to go deeper. We need to go to the root and stop living in denial. These are important steps in our healing.

Through its function of recognition, mind helps us organize and control whatever enters awareness. We like some perceptions and dislike others, so we see what we want to see, hear what we want to hear, and so on. Eye consciousness, ear consciousness, nose consciousness, tongue consciousness, and body consciousness all bring us a modicum of control. That's one of the functions of perception. In the present moment, mind offers us whatever we want to see or hear, even if—at best—it's distorted. To find what's real, we need to look more deeply and touch raw mind.

In raw mind, profound stillness is everywhere, even in noise. Most spirituality teaches us to find stillness in silence. The real work is to find stillness in noise. A silent retreat can help create space in us and temporarily heal our suffering, but our suffering will come back when we return to the noisy world. We need to find stillness in the noise—the noise around us and the noise we receive through mind. Our roots are silent; even the unborn can touch this silence. Raw mind is the heart of mind. Without touching raw mind, we never experience true freedom.

APP 22

Am I Free?

Practice mindful breathing for five minutes. Then say silently, *I am free*. Do this for ten minutes and see how you feel.

23

Spirit of the Mountain

Lao Tzu said, "Namelessness is the root of everything." In raw mind, there are no names. Wisdom sees the nameless nature of things. You can't even call form "form." Any separation between form and nonform is created by mind.

The first five consciousnesses help us recognize the outside world of visual forms, sounds, smells, tastes, and sensate touch. Form is a dense manifestation of our five consciousnesses that comes from the depths of mind. In raw mind, it's just a picture without name or meaning. Ultimately nothing has a name. Yes, practicing the Buddha's Eightfold Path can provide a map. But, ultimately there is only raw reality. In that sense there is no math and no path. To *be peace*, we just need to tune in to ourselves—to the peace frequency.

When I was twenty-five, I visited North Vietnam for the first time. I had left my country fourteen years earlier, but I'd never been to the North. I was on a small boat going to the Perfume Pagoda, the inner sanctuary of a compound of Buddhist shrines, and as we approached the beautiful Huong Tich Mountains with their chalky white limestone, I felt a profound sense of gratitude arise in me. *Rooting was taking place*. Although I was seeing the mountain for the first time, it felt as if I'd been there before, perhaps thousands of years ago.

Throughout the world, indigenous peoples feel the presence of spirits in mountains, trees, and all of nature. We're surrounded by spirits, surrounded by life wherever we are. Mindfulness is not just tuning in to the material and the psychological dimensions. We can also feel the spirit of things. To overcome the Cartesian split between mind and matter, mind and body, to transcend the biblical injunction to dominate the earth, we need to reconnect with the world's many spirits. The world is teeming with life.

Am I the Spirit of the Mountain?

Practice mindful breathing for five minutes. Then say silently, *I feel the spirit of life in my heart*. Do this for ten minutes and feel the depths within yourself and your connection with all beings.

24

Birth and Death

We are all marching in the direction of death. This "death" is both real and symbolic. It can mean the end of one chapter and the beginning of another.

My father passed away when I was fourteen. He got sick and died within two weeks. After he died, I asked aloud, "Where are you, Dad?" and there was silence. No one answered, so I thought he was gone forever. I began to look for him, and I'm still looking for him.

At the same time, I know that when I die, I'll return to my father, my mother, and my ancestors. I came from my parents and I'll go back to them. It's not that my father is someplace waiting until I die. *He is alive in me now*. Life and death are both happening all the time. The

Big Bang took place 13.8 billion years ago, and the Big Bang is still happening in every moment. Every cell in our bodies comes and goes. Our ancestors come and go. Even our consciousness comes and goes. "I am my ancestors" means I contain everything. *I am plural.* My father didn't disappear. If you look at me, you can see him.

Thinking about death helps us grapple with the big questions. You may see yourself as existent now and think that when you die, you'll become nonexistent. This is only a view—and like all views, it's not real. You coexist with all other beings now, and you will coexist with all beings forever. You are the whole cosmos—the earth, the sunshine, the stars, and the rain. You are the forest, the sky, and the mountain.

Seeing time as moving from past to present to future is naive. Time doesn't move; our mind moves. If I say my father is gone, I'm caught by my mind. Nothing can "go." When we look in this way, we understand intergenerational suffering and multigenerational joy. We *are* those who have come before and those not yet born. We may not yet see the faces of our descendants, but they are already in us. Even if you never have children, the future is in you too.

Am I the Whole Cosmos?

Practice mindful breathing for five minutes. Then say silently, *I can see life and death as one*. Do this for ten minutes. Do you feel more settled within?

25

Roots

As we grow older, we begin to think about our *roots*. Roots may be symbolized by where we were born or the place our ancestors came from. In a deeper sense, roots transcend birth, death, and space. We may think we're isolated, but "it takes a village" to support each life. We are all together on Earth Island. Like fantastic fungi, we are connected to ourselves and each other by deep threads.

When the Buddha sensed his own death was coming, he began a long walk north toward the place where he was born, Lumbini. Dying entails going home. A tree returns to the earth as its source, and we too return to our Mother Earth. We must honor our planet and treat the earth with respect, so that we and future generations can return ourselves and our planet to health. We are members of the same family on an evolutionary journey, and we need to live wisely.

Twenty years after my father died, my mother had a stroke. I sat at her bedside and sang "Breathing In and Breathing Out" until she fell asleep. She stayed in bed for seven years. I was a monk when I learned that she was passing away, and I returned to Holland to be with her. I reminded her about her father, my grandpa. She had often talked about him; she loved him dearly. He was a medicine man in their village in Vietnam, using herbs and other natural remedies to help people who were ill, and the villagers loved him. He loved his youngest daughter, my mother, the most.

When I talked to her about her father, peace came to her eyes. I could see it and feel it. In her last moments, she couldn't speak, but she could hear everything. She was happy she was going to see him. That was her way of returning to her roots. We all need a dimension where we can embrace both life and death. Without rootedness, we feel fragile and lonely. When we find our roots, we're no longer a solitary individual but a part of something greater.

I told my mother in her last days that I will eat, walk, laugh, and cry for her. I told her that if she looks deeply into me, she will see herself. Looking into the past, she was able to see her father. Looking into the future, she saw her son. We're not only in the present; we are also our ancestors and all future generations.

One day at Plum Village, I was drinking tea with Thich Nhat Hanh and he told me, "You are my continuation." I replied, "And you are my continuation." He was surprised by my statement and so was I. It had come so quickly. Now I understand I meant there is no distance between us. I am my teacher; my teacher is in me. It's a wonderful feeling to have your teacher in you wherever you are. I felt like a tree that has found its roots. Wherever the tree is, the roots are there. Roots make a tree solid, able to withstand many storms.

APP 25

Am I My Ancestors?

Practice mindful breathing for five minutes. Then say silently, *I am my ancestors*, for ten minutes. Do you feel more connected to the universe and all beings? You may also try, *I am future generations*.

26

Cloud of Wisdom

No one can say, "I will live forever." We're all dying. Death makes us all equal. We all return to the earth and to the sky. At my mother's cremation, I was standing outside and I saw her smoke come out the chimney and rise to the clouds. *Mom, you're now a cloud*, I thought.

Take a good look at yourself, or anyone. We are all clouds, too. There's no need to wait. We have always been clouds.

When I was a monk visiting Vietnam, I met a famous writer who had known Thich Nhat Hanh as a young man. He talked and talked, then he offered me a piece of fruit I'd never had before. So I asked, "What is this?" He knew that I lived in Europe, so he didn't think the question strange, and he answered, "This is jackfruit." Then he went on talking. I could feel that he wasn't in the moment, that he was so excited about seeing a student of Thich Nhat Hanh that he was caught in his ordinary mind, unable to access his cloud of wisdom.

See yourself as a cloud. For that, you need concentration. Without being focused, you may be guided by manas. When we are driven by manas, we perceive everything through thoughts and concepts. To see yourself as a cloud does not require knowledge of anything; it is wisdom.

I asked the writer three more times, "What is this?" but he didn't understand. He continued to say, "This is jackfruit." It's not that he'd answered incorrectly. It was not a Zen master offering a *kung-an*, or koan. It was that he was caught by manas and unable to be present with me. I could have shared a lot about my teacher, but he wasn't really there.

We go through life with knowledge—concepts and ideas—and rarely touch life. We live with someone for ten, twenty, fifty years, and we never see them. Love is not something to be taken for granted. The other person still lives with us and spends long days beside us. But until we *feel* their love, we won't know them, or the meaning of life. When we discover the rawness of this moment, we will feel only gratitude. When we realize how much we receive, we will want to give back.

Wisdom helps us understand life and death. Knowledge cannot. Knowledge is mind. It's great at processing data, but it can't understand life as a whole. Wisdom embraces wholeness. Wisdom is raw mind.

APP 26
Am I a Cloud?

Practice mindful breathing for five minutes. Then say silently, *I am a white cloud in the blue sky. I embody wisdom and freedom in my being.* Do this for ten minutes. These fifteen minutes will bring you stability and joy. Do you feel the presence of the blue sky in your mind?

27

Death Gives
Life Meaning

A Dutch elementary school teacher taught me the importance of putting a period at the end of each sentence. He reminded me again and again, and thanks to his persistence, I learned to write sentences. A sentence without a period has no meaning. It would be like a life without a death. Life and death inter-are. There can be no life without a period, a "full stop" at the end.

Ten years ago, a woman came to me after I'd given a lecture and said, "Cuong, I have only three months to live." She cried, and I did too. I paused and then told her she could still enjoy every day of her life. On the spot, I taught her conscious breathing and said I believed that she could touch life deeply, day after day, no matter how long she had.

And I taught her the art of generosity (*dana paramita*). At some point, we have to let go of everything, even our body. We get sick, and we die. Illness gives health meaning. Death gives life meaning. No matter how careful we are about staying healthy, sooner or later, we will get sick and die. All that remains is what we give now. Everything else disappears. Through giving and forgiving, we discover and enjoy life.

She listened attentively, and in her last days she gave everything she had. She gave her presence. She gave her support, and she forgave, too. Thanks to that focus, she discovered the beauty of a life of giving. She outlived her doctor's expectations. And after three years, she died peacefully. She had rented a quiet hotel room in Greece, where she could hear the sound of the waves. There, she let go of her body and mind. She enjoyed her final days so much, she felt that she had discovered the meaning of life.

If you see yourself only as an individual, life may seem meaningless. If you see yourself as living at a certain moment in history or in a certain phase of your life, you might also experience meaninglessness. If you think we simply come into this world and then we go, that we're born and then we die, you are seeing only the surface dimension—not the root dimension. Without touching your roots, you miss life's texture and depth. You are *all of life*. If you see yourself as whole, you will be able to help others.

The meaning of life reveals itself when you help others. It doesn't matter how proficient you are at taking care of yourself; you can't be completely happy if you don't recognize the community of humans and nonhumans of which we are a part. If you think you're separate, an individual, you won't want to let go of your body or mind. You will fear death.

Know that you are whole. You *are* the root. You don't begin to exist at a certain moment and cease to exist in another. The idea of *creation* is born from a wrong view that you are an individual. You aren't. No one on this beautiful planet is alone or unimportant. Look deeply at others and you'll see how wonderful they are, too. Even after they make mistakes in their life, they're still remarkable, and you are connected to them and to the stars. If you see yourself as created, you won't understand interconnection.

When the wind blows fiercely, a tree needs strong roots to stand firm. Especially in difficult moments, we need roots. Roots help us remember that we're more than we think. We can learn to connect with our roots in daily life. Use your imagination to see that you are your father, your mother, and all your ancestors in this moment. When you touch raw mind, you touch the root dimension and the wholeness of yourself.

Clean water, healthy food, and clean air cannot be taken for granted. With mindfulness, we can see the beauty of life and the meaning of death. We live and discover life's gifts—our neighbor, the tulips and the roses, the clouds in the sky. They are all miracles. Sometimes we only realize that life is precious when we lose someone or something. The greatest pain is to die without actually living.

What is the meaning of life? For me it's a discovery, moment by moment. And to discover anything, we use our wisdom, not our ideas. We have to learn to live, and we can do that while we are alive. And when we discover the deep meaning of life, we discover the deep meaning of death at the same time. Death makes life possible. Death gives meaning to life.

We belong to the family of life, and we accept each other wholeheartedly. We needn't judge or discriminate. With this understanding, we can stop wars and reverse climate change. We can make the earth more beautiful. This is all within reach, and the starting point is seeing your roots, your *connection* to all beings. When you discover raw mind, you'll know that you are whole. This is the realm of unconditional love.

I invite you to discover your life, discover the meaning of life. Through that discovery, you'll become a free person. Death is not our enemy. Suffering is not our enemy. Death is part of life, just as suffering has an important role to play in happiness.

APP 27

Am I All Living Beings?

Practice mindful breathing for five minutes. Then say silently, *I am all beings—past, present, and future*, for ten minutes. Can you feel the richness within?

28

Unified World

Mind separates the world into inside and outside. The inside world and the outside world are both made of images. Even "the world" is a representation. All day long, our senses work in concert with mind. When we dream, we touch the inside world.

Trauma is a product of mind. A shock enters our nervous system and stays there. Mind stores its meaning, and that influences our perceptions. We are on full alert, heeding danger signals triggered by trauma-affected perceptions. Suffering holds on tightly. Mindfulness can bring relief, but what is most effective is the presence of another person who doesn't think the way we do, someone who is in touch with raw mind.

As a prison chaplain, I witnessed the transformation of prisoners who had suffered throughout their lives. I didn't do anything; that was the key. The more we try to help, the more we reinforce the paradigm of suffering, which after a point only makes things worse. By doing nothing, by returning back to my own raw mind, my own roots, I was able to help the inmates return to theirs. We sat together, and we breathed. This is coregulation. Coming back to raw mind—*doing nothing*—we reattune at a frequency different from the one created by mind.

There is a *unified world* that is neither inside nor outside. I'd sit with prisoners for about twenty minutes, and we'd both get in touch with this unified world. And when we did, the inside world would stop for a while, which was enough to bring peace and, sometimes, transformation. We believe the inside world is real, but it isn't. It too is a product of mind. To get relief from our anguish, we need a new perspective. In the unified world, we feel the presence of raw mind. Manas and mind consciousness stop leading your life. You are at home in the world, nourished by the energy of raw mind.

Am I at Home?

Practice mindful breathing for five minutes. Then say silently, *I am in the unified world. I am at home, and I feel at peace.* Do this for ten minutes. Do you feel safe and at ease?

29

Raw Mind

There are times we simply feel hopeless. We've lost everything we love, and we're standing in total emptiness. We feel powerless. When someone you love is about to die, you may feel powerless. These moments are painful, but they are important for us to discover something that has been beyond our reach. If we don't know the feeling of overwhelm, we cannot grow. When everything proceeds according to our internal "script," we tend to be complacent.

When I learned that my father had died, I had that kind of feeling. He had been hospitalized just two weeks earlier, and my sister ran into my room and said, "Dad is dead." I was too young to understand. What did it mean?

Why? I had visited him the day before. My mother had said, "Cuong is here, honey," and he nodded. He recognized me, and I thought, *He's very sick, but he's going to get better*. My father was a big support for me in a strange country. Then he left without even saying goodbye. He was unable to speak, and when my sister said, "Dad is dead," I didn't know what it meant. The next day, his body was there in a coffin, but that wasn't my dad. No one could bring him back.

That was my second big loss. My first was when we had to flee Vietnam. I was losing my friends, my teachers, and also my identity. When you tear a child from their environment, they may lose their identity. I came to Holland where people didn't speak my language and saw me as a stranger, a refugee. It was all very scary.

The pain of a child who has lost himself is unfathomable. To lose all the things you love and know that you'll never see them again is a kind of death. On the boat leaving Vietnam, I looked around and saw only the ocean, no land at all. One big wave, and we'd all die. That was my first experience with death—the death of my identity and all that I loved. In the holding center in Hong Kong, I watched my relatives being treated like animals, beaten, despised. I got really sick and almost died. I felt so hopeless, and no one seemed to understand. They just thought I was weak or that the conditions were unsanitary. But I was sick inside. A part of me had died.

Being so lost, not knowing who you are, is painful. And it is pivotal for growth. And I think we all get opportunities like this, representing our own death or the death of an important chapter of our life. The moment you hear you're dying, you may wonder, "Who am I, actually?" And at that moment, you understand the feeling I had as an eleven-year-old.

You might say, "You were too sensitive." I don't know, but after that journey, I was no longer a child. Through suffering, I had suddenly grown. Then, at the age of twenty-five, I decided to become a monk, because I had met someone who had found himself. Who was he? I wanted to find out. And I want you to find your identity, to find yourself. What you think of as "yourself" might not be you. And when you have not touched your own essence, you won't be able to see others.

When you wake up in the morning, you have a body. You walk with it, eat with it, have sex with it. And at the moment of death, you must let go of it, and you wish there were something you could take with you. You can take your soul, but what does that mean? What part of your soul can you take with you? The good part?

At the moment you know you have to let go of everything, there may be enormous peace, no more fighting. You accept your loss. For some people, this is the moment of enlightenment. You look around and suddenly you find everything simply beautiful. For the first time, you can let go of your ego. You look at others and suddenly discover who they are. Until that moment, you've looked at other people through an "I," your judgments. When you look at others without an "I," you can accept them as they are, with no judgments, and you can see yourself.

After thirty years of mindfulness practice, I've learned that all mental activities have the same value, and we need to respect them all. They are all new and can be appreciated with wisdom and openness. If we discriminate against any mind state, we are discriminating against ourselves.

Now I'm married, and my wife and I are the proud parents of three children. From time to time, she asks, "Are you happy?" and I say, "Yes, I'm very happy." And I know I still have a path in front of me.

Still, looking into the future, I have hope. I know that true life will never end. Life has a home just as a tree has roots. We all share the same roots, which are present in raw mind. When you can see yourself completely, thanks to discovering your roots, you will see how beautiful you are, how beautiful others are, and how beautiful life is. Don't divide yourself in a battlefield. You are wonderful exactly as you are.

Am I Compassion?

Practice mindful breathing for five minutes. Then say silently, *I know there is compassion in my heart*, for ten minutes. You might even taste the power of emptiness and nondiscrimination.

30

Bringing the Practice Home

When I was a monk, I loved to bake bread for the community. Thich Nhat Hanh knew how much I loved to bake, and one day he said to me, "We need to realize our enlightenment exactly the way you bake bread. We know what ingredients we need and how to put them together in the right quantities and timing. We need to know exactly what to do to touch enlightenment." That was an important instruction for me, and I looked at him with gratitude. In his books and public talks, he rarely spoke about enlightenment. He said, "A child asked me, 'Are you enlightened?' and I replied, 'Of course, I am. That's why I'm your teacher.'" He laughed as he told me this.

There are many ways to integrate the practice of mindful living and cultivate raw mind. In this book I offer thirty apps you can practice at any time. You can slice vegetables mindfully or use a bell (or a cuckoo clock, a timer, or even a helicopter with buckets dumping water on a forest fire) to prompt mindfulness.

Here is another practice you can do all the time. It's the practice I loved the most while training at Plum Village. Thich Nhat Hanh would say, "In Plum Village, we have only one way of walking—walking meditation." I could practice mindful walking all day long and get in touch with the energy of mindfulness. I felt a happiness in my body and my mind, and it freed me from all my thoughts. When I told this to Thich Nhat Hanh, he suggested, "Make that energy solid."

One day when I was returning to my room after walking in meditation, I could feel my whole body surrounded by a peaceful light. I looked up and saw Thich Nhat Hanh, and he smiled. You can practice mindful walking anytime, indoors or outdoors. You might try saying silently with each step, *In*, as you breathe in and *Out*, as you breathe out. Be creative. There are many ways you can bring your attention inward and stay present with your sensations, emotions, breath, and even thoughts.

Sometimes at Plum Village when we practiced walking meditation as a community, we experienced a peaceful energy and became deeply quiet within. One time the energy was so serene that Thich Nhat Hanh chose a place in the woods to sit down, and everyone sat with him. The practice of walking meditation transformed into the practice of sitting meditation. In most Zen practice, sitting is at the heart. At Plum Village, I'd say that walking was the heart of the practice. We listened to the bell and we walked, and in every step, we touched peace.

During one question-and-answer session, I said to Thich Nhat Hanh, "Yesterday, I was able to touch freedom during walking meditation. Today, I couldn't. What can I do to free myself from attachment to a past experience?"

Thich Nhat Hanh asked, "Was touching freedom yesterday a pleasant experience?" and I replied, "Yes." And he said, "Then live happily with your pleasant experience. It doesn't have to be an obstacle."

There is a relationship between mind and breath. The practice of conscious breathing is supported by our mind. And our mind is supported by our breathing. When your mind is a mind of discrimination, your practice of breathing cannot be very deep. When you discover raw mind, whether walking, sitting, standing, or lying down, you have a lot of space in yourself, and your breathing will flow more easily.

Conscious breathing brings you home. It helps your true mind transform your suffering. Raw mind doesn't discriminate, so it can make it easier to recognize beauty. One day, you wake up and notice that your suffering has been transformed. You don't know how or when it happened. Like compost in soil, it's been embraced by the earth's wisdom of nondiscrimination and transformed into a beautiful flower garden. It wasn't exactly mindful breathing that transformed suffering. We don't practice to transform or control anything or to seek the good or overcome evil. Both good and evil need to be embraced by love. That is raw mind, transformation at the base.

APP 30

Am I True Happiness?

Practice mindful breathing for five minutes. Then say silently, *I open my heart to allow true happiness to find me*. Do this for ten minutes. Do you feel more open and at ease?

AFTERWORD
A Note about Buddhist Psychology

At Plum Village, I specialized in Buddhist psychology. I admired the way Thich Nhat Hanh taught Buddhist psychology and especially the way he put it into practice. Buddhist psychology describes how the mind works, but it's often difficult to apply. Thich Nhat Hanh made it easier to bring into daily life. I hope the apps in this book help you apply the teachings. With mindfulness, we can recognize our mental activities and have an awakened perspective on our mind states as they arise.

The roots of this book are in the Yogachara school of Buddhism. Fourth-century Buddhist master Vasubandhu, who was a prominent figure in the development of Mahayana (Great Vehicle) Buddhism, is said to be a cofounder of the Yogachara school. He was the author of seven works on Buddhist psychology, and it was he who posited eight consciousnesses—the five sense consciousnesses, mind consciousness (manovijnana), manas, and store consciousness (alayavijnana).

We usually identify with our body and our consciousness. Buddhist psychology helps us understand the dynamics of this, let go of attachment to the eight consciousnesses, and discover raw mind, which is our true mind, our true self, the heart of our being. Ordinary mind is based on concepts. Raw mind cannot be conceptualized. Reading this book and practicing the apps, I hope you will discover ways to get in touch with your true self and your true mind. That is the greatest happiness.

I founded Mind Only–Institute for Buddhist Psychology, based in the Netherlands, so I could teach traditional Buddhist psychology and introduce raw mind. Without understanding raw mind, we are caught in the stories we tell ourselves. When I found raw mind, I discovered you. Your mind is my mind, your happiness is my happiness, your freedom is my freedom.

Vasubandhu wrote the *Trimsika Vijnaptimatrata* (Thirty Verses on Consciousness Only) to explain the eight consciousnesses and how we can free ourselves of them. My interpretative translation follows. See especially verse 29, where Vasubandhu describes freeing ourselves of ordinary mind as "transformation at the base."

1. Due to the concepts *self* and *dharmas*, multiple mutual microinteractions are possible. Each of these interactions depends on consciousness to manifest, and there are three kinds of manifestation.

2. The three kinds of manifestation are (a) maturation, (b) mentation (manas), and (c) perception of the sense fields by the sense organs. Maturation, or ripening, refers to the store consciousness (alayavijnana), which stores all the seeds, or potentials, in the form of concepts.

3. Ripening takes place with contact, attention, feeling, perception, and volition. The way this takes place is ultimately unknowable. It does not involve preferences; it involves only neutral feelings.

4. Maturation manifestation is neither obscured nor karmically predetermined. The same is true of contact, attention, feeling, perception, and volition. Maturation is taking place constantly, like the flow of a river. In the state of those who have gained insight into the true nature of existence, it is unencumbered.

5. The second manifestation of consciousness is manas. Dependent on store consciousness, manas turns around and objectifies consciousness. Its nature is mentation.

6. Manas always goes together with the afflictions of self-confusion, self-view, self-arrogance, and self-cherishing. It arises along with contact, attention, feeling, perception, and volition.

7. Manas is obscured and karmically indeterminate. It arises wherever it is born and bound to a self-concept. In the state of perfected insight, the cessation of manas is complete. On the supramundane path, manas no longer exists.

8. The third manifestation of consciousness is perception of the sense fields by the sense organs. This is of six types—seeing, hearing, smelling, tasting, tactile sensation, and thought—and its nature is of discerning objects. They can be good, bad, or neither—wholesome, unwholesome, or neutral.

9. Perception consciousness is associated with mental formations like the universals, the specifics, the beneficials, the afflictions, and the secondary

afflictions and interacts with all three kinds of feelings (pleasant, unpleasant, neutral).

10. The universals are contact, attention, feeling, perception, and volition. (These formations are totally different in the three kinds of manifestations: maturation, mentation, and perception of the sense fields by the sense organs.) The specifics are desire, confidence, memory, concentration, and wisdom.

11. The beneficials are faith, shame, embarrassment, generosity, loving-kindness, wisdom, diligence, ease, care, equanimity, and peace.

12. The afflictions are greed, hatred, ignorance, arrogance, doubt, and wrong views. The secondary afflictions are anger, enmity, hypocrisy, cruel speech, envy, selfishness, . . .

13. deceit, guile, injury, conceit, shamelessness, indignity, restlessness, brain fog, unfaithfulness, sloth, carelessness, forgetfulness, distraction, and lack of discernment.

14. The four indeterminates are remorse, torpor, initial mental application, and sustained discursive thought. These can be beneficial or unbeneficial.

15. Depending on root consciousness, the five consciousnesses arise according to conditions. Sometimes they function separately and sometimes together, as waves depend on water.

16. Manovijnana is always working, except in a non-conceptual state, and in the two no-mind concentrations, in sleep and in total unconsciousness.

17. When these consciousnesses manifest, they discriminate and are discriminated against. Because both are empty, it is entirely only consciousness.

18. Consciousness is the totality of the seeds. It manifests in many ways. Through the power of sequential unfolding, it constructs each thing differently.

19. Due to the habit energy of actions and the duality of grasper and grasped, yet another karmic fruit will arise after an earlier fruit has been consumed or depleted.

20. Due to construction after construction, there are multiple constructed objects. There is no such thing as constructed self-nature, however.

21. Interdependent self-nature is cognized by discernment. Self-realization is possible only when

the interdependent and the constructed are distinguished.

22. Therefore, this self-nature and its interdependent nature are neither different nor not different, just as it is with an impermanent object and *its* self-nature. If you cannot see one, you cannot see the other.

23. Contingent on these self-natures, the three non-natures are established. Thus the Buddha taught that nothing has a self-nature.

24. The first non-nature is so because of its very nature. The second is so because it cannot be by itself alone. The third is so because of the very state of the absence of self-nature.

25. The ultimate nature of all dharmas is also *suchness*. Its nature is always just as it is. This is the very meaning of the mind only.

26. As long as your consciousness has not reached the state of mind only, traces of dualistic grasping will always be present.

27. You may experience a tiny insight and say, "This is mind only." But since your experience still has an object, it is not the state of mind only.

28. If you see that you can't *grasp* the object of your

consciousness, you are abiding in mind only.
When there is no object to grasp, there is no
longer grasping.

29. In the state of unthinkable, ungraspable supramundane wisdom, nothing can be attained or
acquired. Letting go of this twofold impedi-
ment, transformation at the base is realized.

30. This is called the Dharma of the Great Sage, the
immaculate, inconceivable, beneficent, con-
stant, blissful body of liberation.

FURTHER READING ABOUT
BUDDHIST PSYCHOLOGY

Goodman, Steven D. *The Buddhist Psychology of Awakening: An In-Depth Guide to Abhidharma*. Boulder, CO: Shambhala Publications, 2020.

Jacobs, Beth. *The Original Buddhist Psychology: What the Abhidharma Tells Us about How We Think, Feel, and Experience Life*. Berkeley, CA: North Atlantic Books, 2017.

Kornfield, Jack. *The Wise Heart: A Guide to the Universal Teachings of Buddhist Psychology*. New York: Bantam Books, 2008.

Narada Mahathera and Bhikkhu Bodhi. *A Comprehensive Manual of Abhidhamma: The Abhidhammattha Sangaha of Acariya Anuruddha*. Onalaska, WA: BPS Pariyatti Editions, 2020.

Nhat Hanh, Thich. *The Heart of the Buddha's Teaching: Transforming Suffering into Peace, Joy, and Liberation*. New York: Broadway Books, 1998.

———. *Understanding Our Mind*. Berkeley, CA: Parallax Press, 2008.

Vasubandhu, *Abhidharmakosabhasyam*. Translated into
French by Louis De La Vallee Poussin and into English by
Leo M. Pruden. 4 vols. Fremont, CA: Asian Humanities
Press, 1990.

ABOUT THE AUTHOR

PHOTO BY MERLIJN DOOMERNIK

CUONG LU, Buddhist teacher, scholar, and writer, was born in Nha Trang, Vietnam, in 1968 and emigrated to the Netherlands with his family in 1980. He majored in East Asian studies at the University of Leiden, and in 1993 was ordained a monk at Plum Village in France under the guidance of Thich Nhat Hanh. In 2000, he was recognized as a teacher in the Lieu Quan line of the Linji School of Zen Buddhism.

In 2009, Cuong left Plum Village after sixteen years and returned to lay life in the Netherlands. He served as a chaplain in Holland's penitentiary system for six years.

In 2015, he received a master's degree in Buddhist spiritual care at Vrije Universiteit in Amsterdam.

Cuong is the founder of Mind Only, located in Gouda, where he teaches Buddhist philosophy and psychology, specializing in Yogachara Buddhism combined with the Madhyamaka (middle way) school of Nagarjuna. In 2022, he founded the No Word Zen order, emphasizing the whole world as a place of practice. Cuong leads retreats and gives Dharma talks in Europe, the United States, and Asia and offers presentations to large organizations. He is the author of *The Buddha in Jail: Restoring Lives, Finding Hope and Freedom* and *Wait: A Love Letter to Those in Despair*. Visit mindonly.org and nowordzen.com.